ANCESTRAL VOICES
a family story

A R Gurney

BROADWAY PLAY PUBLISHING INC
New York
www.broadwayplaypublishing.com
info@broadwayplaypublishing.com

Cover art by Jim McMullan

First edition: March 2000
This edition: April 2018
I S B N: 978-0-88145-171-9

Book design: Marie Donovan
Copy editing, 2000: Liam Brosnahan
Page make-up: Adobe InDesign
Typeface: Palatino

The first reading of ANCESTRAL VOICES was at the Lincoln Center Theater on 15 September 1998. The cast was:

EDDIE .... David Aaron Baker
JANE .... Debra Monk
HARVEY .... James Rebhorn
GRANDMOTHER .... Julie Harris
GRANDFATHER .... Mason Adams

The official opening of ANCESTRAL VOICES was at the Lincoln Center Theater's Mitzi Newhouse Theater on 18 October 1999. The cast was:

EDDIE .... David Aaron Baker
JANE .... Blythe Danner
HARVEY .... Edward Herrmann
GRANDMOTHER .... Elizabeth Wilson
GRANDFATHER .... Philip Bosco

My thanks to all the other actors along the way, and to Daniel Sullivan for directing

CHARACTERS

EDDIE, *younger*
JANE, EDDIE's *mother*
HARVEY, EDDIE's *father*
EDDIE's GRANDMOTHER *(and* MRS MITCHELL*); older*
EDDIE's GRANDFATHER *(and* UNCLE ROGER*); older*

This play is designed to be read aloud by five actors—three men and two women of various ages—using chairs and music stands placed so as to provide the best sight lines. The stands should mask the scripts as much as possible. The play also seems to work best if the actors do not look at each other as they read, except toward the end, where indicated. Otherwise, they should focus more towards the audience, thereby including them in the event.

COSTUMES

Men: EDDIE *might wear a sweater and open shirt;* HARVEY, *a dark business suit;* GRANDFATHER, *a sports jacket and gray flannels with tie.*

Women: JANE, *a dark dress or dark formal slacks;* GRANDMOTHER, *a dark dress.*

SET

A stage of any kind. Possibly different kinds of antique chairs to reflect the characters of the older actors. A simple desk chair for EDDIE. *No intermission is needed.*

For André Bishop with love and appreciation

(At rise:)

(The four older actors enter first, followed by EDDIE. *All are carrying their scripts. The others sit, put their scripts on their music stands, open them.* EDDIE *remains standing.)*

EDDIE: *(To audience)* This started to be a play, but it went too many places for the stage.

GRANDMOTHER: *(Reading)* Come out to the country and see me, Eddie!

EDDIE: So it tried to be a book, but people kept wanting to talk.

GRANDFATHER: *(Reading)* Let me tell you about trout, Eddie…

EDDIE: So the only thing to do…

HARVEY: *(Reading)* Get in the car, Eddie!

EDDIE: Is take the best of both worlds…

JANE: *(Reading)* Hurry, sweetheart. Hop in back.

EDDIE: *(Sitting, joining the others)* And sit down and read it out loud. *(Opens script)* We were in my father's new, battleship-grey, 1938 LaSalle convertible, driving out to the country, to see my grandparents in their weekend cottage, near Buffalo, New York, where I was born. My father was driving….

HARVEY: Settle down back there, children. Your mother wants to tell you something.

EDDIE: My mother was looking out the window.

HARVEY: They seem all keyed up.

JANE: Maybe they sense something.

EDDIE: My sister Nancy was singing, "To grandmother's house we go…" And my little brother Tim was counting cows. *(Imitating Tim)* Thirteen…fourteen…fifteen… *(As if to Tim)* You're getting boring, Timmy.

HARVEY: Children, pay attention. Something's come up.

EDDIE: *(To HARVEY)* Tim's counting cows.

HARVEY: Don't count cows for a minute, Tim. *(To JANE)* Go ahead, darling.

JANE: I can't, Harvey. I'll cry.

HARVEY: Shall I do the honors then?

JANE: No, no. I'll do it. This is about my mother, not yours.

HARVEY: I won't argue with that.

JANE: Kids, listen. Do you remember a man named Mr Woodrich?

EDDIE: I do. He won the silver cup with Gramp.

JANE: That's exactly right, Eddie. When your grandfather won the golf tournament last year, Mr Woodrich was his partner.

EDDIE: They won a big silver cup. I was there, and Nancy and Tim weren't.

HARVEY: Just listen to your mother, Eddie.

EDDIE: Tim's counting cows again.

HARVEY: That's enough cows for a while, Timmy boy.

JANE: Here's the thing, kids: when we get to your grandmother's, Mr Woodrich will be there.

HARVEY: Uncle Roger. Your grandmother wants you to call him Uncle Roger.

EDDIE: Why uncle? *(To audience)* We have a lot of uncles already.

JANE: You have a new Uncle now. You have Uncle Roger.

EDDIE: Timmy's now counting uncles.

HARVEY: That's enough counting, Tim.

EDDIE: Is he a real uncle?

JANE: No, he is not. But you have to pretend that he is.

EDDIE: Is she going to marry him?

JANE: I guess that's pretty much up to him.

HARVEY: Of course she'll marry him. You can't live in Buffalo and not be married.

EDDIE: I thought she was married to Gramp.

JANE: I thought she was, too, Eddie. And I thought Mr Woodrich was married to Mrs Woodrich. I thought a lot of things I no longer think.

HARVEY: Your grandparents have decided to separate.

JANE: After all these years of marriage.

EDDIE: What's separate mean?

HARVEY: It means they don't want to be with each other any more. It boils down to that.

JANE: *(To* HARVEY*)* It means she doesn't want to be with Father. How Father feels is a very different matter.

HARVEY: I don't think we need to get into all that.

JANE: Oh I hate this. I loathe it. I'd like to turn right around and drive straight back to town.

HARVEY: Every family has a hole in it somewhere, darling. Our job is to fill it up.

EDDIE: What about Gramp?

JANE: Exactly, Eddie. That's the sixty-four dollar question. What about him?

HARVEY: Time heals all wounds.

JANE: You and your Shakespeare.

HARVEY: I'm not sure that's Shakespeare.

JANE: I hope it isn't. It's too trite to be Shakespeare.

HARVEY: Easy now, Jane. Just take it easy.

EDDIE: Will Gramp be there? When we get there?

HARVEY: Foolish question number nine hundred and ninety-nine.

JANE: I'm afraid he won't be, poor soul.

EDDIE: I was looking forward to asking him things. I want to ask him things about salmon.

HARVEY: Well you can't, that's all.

EDDIE: It's for a composition. For school.

JANE: We'll see your grandfather some other time, Eddie. Today we have to sit around and stare at Uncle Roger.

HARVEY: Roger Woodrich has a great deal of charm.

JANE: Apparently.

HARVEY: All the Woodriches do. A great deal of charm and a great deal of money. Sometimes the two things go together.

JANE: Apparently they do.

HARVEY: Of course there's charm and there's charm. And there's money and there's—

EDDIE: *(Interrupting)* Could we stop and see Gramp later?

HARVEY: Eddie, I believe you were interrupting.

JANE: Good idea, Eddie! We'll stop by later.

HARVEY: The boy was interrupting my train of thought, Jane.

JANE: But it's Sunday. We should see Father.

EDDIE: I love Gramp. *(To audience)* I'm even named after him. He's Ed, I'm Eddie. *(To* JANE*)* Gramp's my favorite person, Mom.

JANE: I know exactly how you feel, Eddie. *(To* HARVEY*)* She's thinking of buying a horse, you know.

EDDIE: Nancy shouted again: "Buying a HORSE? A real HORSE?"

JANE: Please don't yell in my ear, Nancy… But yes, your grandmother has decided she likes horseback riding.

HARVEY: Roger Woodrich is a magnificent rider.

JANE: What's that supposed to mean?

HARVEY: It means he rides well. That's all it means.

JANE: Horseback-riding is the culprit in all this. If they hadn't started riding together…

EDDIE: Tell us about the horse.

JANE: Ask your grandmother. She's the big rider these days.

EDDIE: I'll ask her why she doesn't like Gramp any more.

HARVEY: Don't, Eddie. Just plain don't.

JANE: I almost wish he would.

HARVEY: I'll bet he does. Just to cause trouble.

JANE: Don't do it, Eddie. We might want to, but we can't.

HARVEY: And…here we are… And there is your grandmother waiting at the door!

GRANDMOTHER: Hello! …Hello, everyone!

EDDIE: Where's— *(Whispering to* HARVEY*)* What do we call him again?

HARVEY: *(Whispering)* Uncle Roger.

GRANDMOTHER: Everybody give me a big kiss! Mmmm… Mmmm… Now, children, run into the house, and say hello to your Uncle Roger.

HARVEY: Look him right in the eye.

GRANDMOTHER: Yes, and give him a good firm handshake, and call him by name.

HARVEY: Say "Welcome to the family, Uncle Roger."

GRANDMOTHER: Thank you, Harvey. I appreciate that. And so will Roger.

JANE: *(Softly)* This is an absolute nightmare.

***

GRANDMOTHER: Eddie, come over here to the sideboard, and help me pour the tomahto juice for the children.

EDDIE: O K.

GRANDMOTHER: *(Confidingly)* Tell me. Do you like him?

EDDIE: Who?

GRANDMOTHER: Who? Your Uncle Roger, you silly billy.

EDDIE: I guess.

GRANDMOTHER: You guess? Didn't you speak to him?

EDDIE: I did, but he didn't speak back. He just kept on reading the funnies.

GRANDMOTHER: He loves those Sunday funnies.

EDDIE: I guess he does.

GRANDMOTHER: I hope you like him, Eddie.

EDDIE: I hope so, too.

GRANDMOTHER: I hope everyone does. I hope we can make these Sundays a regular thing. Wouldn't you like to come out here every Sunday for a lovely lunch?

EDDIE: I guess.

GRANDMOTHER: You're doing an awful lot of guessing today, aren't you, Eddie?

EDDIE: I guess I am.

***

EDDIE: *(To audience)* After we got back from the country, my Mother and I drove down Delaware Avenue to see my Grandfather in his house on Summer Street.

JANE: See that parking lot, Eddie? That's where the old Irwin house used to be.

EDDIE: *(To audience)* That's the way we talk in Buffalo. We name houses by the people who lived in them.

JANE: Every winter, we all used to take the hose and make a big skating rink in the back yard. Then we'd play ice-tag and crack-the-whip. Afterwards, the Irwins would have us all in for hot chocolate.

EDDIE: (To JANE) The Irwins are building a new home outside of town.

JANE: Never say "home", Eddie. Say "house". A house is a building. A "home" is what happens inside. The Irwins are building a house outside of town. Let's hope they can turn it into a home.

EDDIE: (To audience) My grandfather's house is where my mother grew up. It has all sorts of rooms, upstairs and down. There's a big bedroom reserved just for Congressman Maxwell, who stays there whenever he's not in Washington. If you get a speeding ticket, you just call up Jack Maxwell. And there's also a sunporch for my grandfather's sports trophies and the stuffed animals from his hunting trips to Africa and Alaska.

JANE: How are you, Father?

GRANDFATHER: I'm all right.

EDDIE: (To audience) Gramp drinks Old-Fashioned cocktails and smokes Chesterfield cigarettes.

GRANDFATHER: How about you there, Eddie?

EDDIE: I'm good, Gramp.

GRANDFATHER: Look at these letters, Jane. From my friends throughout the city. Expressing their sympathy and condolences. Want to read them?

JANE: No I don't, Father.

GRANDFATHER: You should read them. They make me glad I have friends.

JANE: You do, Father. You have a great many friends.

GRANDFATHER: Want to read these, Eddie?

JANE: He doesn't want to read them, Father.

EDDIE: I'm not too good at reading older people's writing, Gramp.

GRANDFATHER: I'll save them, so you can read them some day, Eddie. You'll learn a thing or two about life.

EDDIE: Your cigarette ash is falling on the rug, Gramp.

GRANDFATHER: That's all right. Good for the moths.

JANE: Did you do anything about lunch, Father? Did Mrs Driscoll leave something?

EDDIE: (To audience) Mrs Driscoll and Annie are Gramp's maids, but they're Catholics, so on Sundays they go to Mass to see their friends from Ireland.

JANE: I'll bet you haven't had a thing since breakfast. Come and have supper with us.

GRANDFATHER: Did you go out there today?

JANE: She asked us.

GRANDFATHER: Was he there?

JANE: Yes he was, Father.

GRANDFATHER: She wanted that place especially for Sundays.

JANE: I know, Father.

GRANDFATHER: I had a tough time buying that property. Had to call old Judge Landis and pull strings. But when I finally make the deal, when I say "All right. Here you are, Madeleine, here's what you wanted—a weekend place for the family," what does she do but... *(Pause)* Want a drink, Jane?

JANE: No thanks, Father.

GRANDFATHER: Eddie, there might be a bottle of root beer in the ice box.

EDDIE: I'll get it, Gramp. Thanks. *(To audience)* So I got it and came back.

GRANDFATHER: It was the horseback riding that did it, Jane.

JANE: So I hear.

GRANDFATHER: Son of a bitch rides right up to her front door. Puts her on a horse. She likes it. One thing leads to another.

JANE: Don't, Father.

GRANDFATHER: Not my idea of a good time, sitting on some nag. Right, Eddie?

EDDIE: Right, Gramp.

JANE: Eddie, why don't you go out to the sun porch and look at your grandfather's hunting trophies?

EDDIE: I'm still drinking my root beer.

JANE: Finish your root beer out on the sun porch, please.

EDDIE: I want to ask Gramp about salmon. I want to know why they always swim home.

GRANDFATHER: Tell you what, Eddie. Go out to the carriage house and say hello to William McKaye. I believe he's Simonzing my car.

EDDIE: *(To audience)* William McKaye came from Scotland and used to be the coachman for Gramp's father.

JANE: Don't take that glass out of doors, please, Eddie. That happens to be a valuable old goblet. It came from old E G's house down on Delaware.

EDDIE: *(To audience)* That's another thing we do in Buffalo. We call people "old" all the time. Old E G was my great-great-grandfather.

GRANDFATHER: Old E G's house? That glass there? No. That glass came from old S S's house in Cooperstown.

EDDIE: *(To audience)* Old S S was Gramp's father—my great-grandfather. He was the one William worked for.

JANE: The point is, Eddie, it's a valuable glass. So finish your root beer and leave that glass carefully in the sink for Annie.

GRANDFATHER: We'll talk about salmon later, Eddie.

EDDIE: *(To audience)* In the carriage house, I climbed into the front seat of one of the old buggies, and William showed me how to hold the reins. "Have you seen your grandmother?" he said. I said we saw her today. "I taught her to drive a car," William said. "Most of her friends were scared to try, but she wanted to learn. Your grandmother was one lively lady." "Was?" I said. "Still is, William. Maybe she'll come back." But William said he didn't think so. He said once they've flown the coop, you can catch them and put them back on the perch, but they never set easy again.

(Pause)

JANE: Eddie! Time to go! Get in the car.

EDDIE: I want to kiss Gramp goodbye.

JANE: Some other time, Eddie. *(As if to William)* Oh, William. Father's a little…under the weather. And he hasn't had a thing to eat.

EDDIE: "I'll take care of him, Miss," William said. And he went into the house.

***

EDDIE: *(To audience)* Last year, before my grandmother started living with Uncle Roger, my sister and I used to walk over to our grandparents' house for lunch from school. And if Gramp had been shooting, he'd call our school and say we could bring some friends. We'd have duck, or quail, or grouse, or pheasant. Gramp would stand up, and we'd all watch him sharpen his carving knife. Then he'd test the blade carefully on his thumb.

GRANDFATHER: We may now proceed with the operation.

EDDIE: *(To audience)* He'd carve very slowly and carefully, and give each plate to Annie, who would take it around to my grandmother.

GRANDMOTHER: Who does not want fresh green beans? They came all the way from Cooperstown.

GRANDFATHER: Watch how I do this, children. This is the breast. And this is the second joint.

GRANDMOTHER: Don't forget that delicious chestnut stuffing.

GRANDFATHER: And here's what they call the Pope's nose. Who wants a bite of the Pope's nose?

GRANDMOTHER: That's enough, Ed, please. You're making Annie uncomfortable.

EDDIE: *(To audience)* Annie didn't like wisecracks about the Pope.

GRANDFATHER: And this is the wishbone which I'll put aside to dry. What's the dessert today, Madeleine?

GRANDMOTHER: Mrs Driscoll has made a lovely Floating Island.

GRANDFATHER: Ah hah. Floating Island! Then after we've had that, Eddie, select two of your guests to make a wish on the wishbone.

GRANDMOTHER: Nancy, you're responsible for passing the gravy, and Eddie, send around that currant jelly. And I want you all to know Mrs Driscoll made these rolls fresh this very morning.

GRANDFATHER: If anyone bites into a piece of shot, don't worry. It won't kill you.

EDDIE: It killed that duck, though.

GRANDMOTHER: It most certainly did, Eddie. A beautiful mallard duck, with bright green feathers.

GRANDFATHER: Just harvesting nature's crop, Madeleine.

GRANDMOTHER: Oh is that what you're doing? I never was quite sure.

EDDIE: Tell us about your hunting trip to Africa, Gramp. *(To audience)* My grandfather shot lions in Africa, and big-horn sheep in Alaska.

GRANDMOTHER: I've had enough of guns and killing, please. I want to know about school. Is Miss Tilly still there?

EDDIE: Oh boy. She sure is.

GRANDMOTHER: Miss Tilly taught *me*, you know.

GRANDFATHER: Taught me, too, as a matter of fact.

GRANDMOTHER: Is she still trying to get rid of our Buffalo accents? *(She recites with a British accent)* Who killed Cock Robin? I, said the sparrow, with my bow and arrow. I killed Cock Robin.

EDDIE: *(Equally affected)* And there weh, in the same countri, shepheds, abiding in the fields…

EDDIE & GRANDMOTHER: *(Together)* …keeping wawch over their flawks by night.

GRANDFATHER: A toast to Miss Tilly!

EDDIE, GRANDFATHER & GRANDMOTHER: *(Together)* To Miss Tilly!

EDDIE: *(To audience)* And back at school everyone would come up to Nancy and me and beg to have lunch with my grandparents. We were very popular.

***

HARVEY: *(Calling out)* I'm home! Where is everybody? Jane? Tim? Anybody?

EDDIE: *(Calling out)* I'm in the living room, in case anyone's interested! Doing my geography! *(Memorizing)* Maine, Augusta, on the Kennebec…New Hampshire, Concord, on the Merrimac…

HARVEY: Where's your lovely mother?

EDDIE: Taking a bath…Vermont, Montpelier, on the Winooski…

HARVEY: Run upstairs and tell her I am about to make her the finest cocktail in the Western World.

EDDIE: I have to memorize my states, capitals, and streams.

HARVEY: Eddie! When your father asks you to do something, you don't argue, you don't procrastinate. You simply leap to your feet and do it!

EDDIE: O K, O K, I'm going.

JANE: Never mind. Here I am.

HARVEY: How lovely you look, darling.

JANE: Thank you.

HARVEY: You might be interested to know that I've just had a drink with Roger Woodrich.

JANE: You didn't.

EDDIE: Uncle Roger?

HARVEY: I believe I was talking to your mother.

JANE: Don't interrupt, Eddie. If you plan to use the bookcase, fine. But be quiet, please.

HARVEY: He called me at work and asked to meet for a drink.

JANE: Not at the Saturn Club, I hope. Father's there every evening.

HARVEY: We met downtown at the Statler Bar. And had a perfectly nice talk. He wanted to clarify his intentions.

EDDIE: What does that mean?

HARVEY: Eddie, go upstairs and get some work done.

EDDIE: I am working…Rhode Island, Providence, on Narragansett Bay….

JANE: People always work better in their own rooms, Eddie.

EDDIE: (To audience) So I went. Slowly.

HARVEY: He's decided to marry her.

JANE: Decided? How big of him!

HARVEY: Frankly, I thought it might just be a fling.

JANE: He's certainly had plenty of those.

HARVEY: He says they'll get married as soon as they've worked out a prenuptial agreement.

JANE: Knowing Mother, she'll hand him the moon.

EDDIE: (To audience) On the landing, I accidentally dropped my book.

HARVEY: Eddie! I thought I told you to go upstairs!

EDDIE: That's where I'm going!

HARVEY: Then go, please. Right now.

EDDIE: (To audience) Gram and Uncle Roger got married in Mexico. Nobody was invited, and Gram said she didn't even wear a veil.

JANE: (To HARVEY) Sooner or later I'll have to tell Father.

HARVEY: Chad Warren told him last night at the Saturn Club. Took him into the billiard room and spelled the whole thing out.

JANE: How did he take it?

HARVEY: Someone had to drive him home.

JANE: Oh no.

EDDIE: Why didn't he drive himself home?

HARVEY: Where did you come from?

EDDIE: I'm hungry.

JANE: Go tell Mabel we're ready, Eddie.

HARVEY: That boy is an eavesdropper. Every time we sit down for a cocktail, there he is.

JANE: He's interested in Father. He adores him.

HARVEY: Why?

JANE: Why? WHY?

HARVEY: I mean he's a perfectly nice man, but....

JANE: He's a marvelous man! You see his name on plaques all over the city! Tennis, golf, squash, skeet-shooting! He can do anything he sets his mind to.

HARVEY: Except ride horseback.

JANE: He could do that, too. He just doesn't want to.

HARVEY: All right, darling. All right.

***

GRANDMOTHER: Eddie! Guess what, dearie. I have bought a horse! A big, gentle, lovely hunter with an easy gait and a smooth canter. Do you like to ride, Eddie? Do you, Tim?

EDDIE: Tim's scared to ride.

GRANDMOTHER: I used to be. But now it's my favorite thing.

EDDIE: Why?

GRANDMOTHER: Because you're free when you ride. You can go anywhere you want.

EDDIE: Can you jump over fences?

GRANDMOTHER: I'm learning. Your Uncle Roger takes every jump, and I'm trying to follow him.

EDDIE: Aren't you scared you'll fall off?

GRANDMOTHER: Petrified. But that makes it thrilling. It opens up a whole new world. It's certainly better than having to huddle shivering in some duck blind.

EDDIE: I think girls like riding more than boys, Gram.

GRANDMOTHER: Then tell you what. We'll let your sister Nancy do the riding, and you boys can do something else. Because Uncle Roger and I are making some big changes out here. We're redoing the house, and putting in a tennis court and a swimming pool, and a special lawn just for croquet.

EDDIE: Will you put in a trout stream?

GRANDMOTHER: No, dearie. I don't believe we'll do that.

EDDIE: Gramp's taking me trout fishing some time.

GRANDMOTHER: You'll have plenty to do out here, Eddie, without hooking some poor fish.

EDDIE: What if I put some trout in the swimming pool?

GRANDMOTHER: No fish in my pool, please, I never want to see another fish in my life.

EDDIE: You could fish for trout any time you wanted.

GRANDMOTHER: Are you teasing me, Eddie? You are, aren't you?

EDDIE: Sort of.

GRANDMOTHER: Well don't, dearie. Please. These days I've got enough on my mind without people teasing.

***

EDDIE: *(To audience)* I wish this could be a movie so they could show this camp my grandfather has on Big Rock Lake in the Adirondacks. He inherited it from Old S S. It's very wild up there. There's no electricity, which means kerosene lamps, and getting your water from the lake, and having to use an out-house. There are lots of trout in the lake, and deer come down to drink, and once when my mother was a little girl up there, she saw a bear. *(To HARVEY and JANE)* Can I ask Gramp to take me to Big Rock this summer?

HARVEY: I wouldn't.

JANE: It might do Father some good. He hasn't been there since Mother left.

HARVEY: The plumbing is non-existent, Eddie. And it rains incessantly.

JANE: Why don't you want him to go, Harvey?

HARVEY: Because he'd be bored out of his mind, if he's anything like me.

EDDIE: I'm not like you.

HARVEY: I'm beginning to discover that.

JANE: I'll speak to Father.

GRANDFATHER: Big Rock with Eddie? I'd like that.

EDDIE: Yippee!

JANE: Here's a chance for you to light a fire under him, Eddie.

HARVEY: But don't bring up your grandmother.

EDDIE: I won't, Pop. I'm not that dumb.

HARVEY: Sometimes I wonder.

EDDIE: *(To audience)* Gramp and I took Route 20 east. And the farther we got from Buffalo, the more Gramp talked.

GRANDFATHER: See that? That is the old Erie Canal. That canal was built so that goods coming from Europe could come up the Hudson, swing past Albany on to Buffalo, and then onto the Great Lakes and out West. And products from the West came back through Buffalo, on down the Hudson, and all over the world. Old E G was working on a farm when he saw them building that canal. Knew a good thing when he saw it. Put down his plough, moved to Buffalo, married a rich girl, started a bank, got the city to dredge a harbor, helped finance it. Ran for Mayor. Ran for State legislature. Ran for Congress. Won every time. Served in Lincoln's cabinet. Taught Lincoln a thing or two about money.

EDDIE: Did old E G get rich?

GRANDFATHER: Rich as Croesus. The city wanted him to donate a library, but he refused. He said he had already donated his time and services, and saw no further reason to diminish his pile.

EDDIE: *(To audience)* We stopped by a lock, and watched a boat go through.

GRANDFATHER: Just the occasional pleasure boat these days.

EDDIE: *(To audience)* We drove north, past Utica, along West Canada Creek up into the mountains…. *(To GRANDFATHER)* Why are we stopping at this little cemetery?

GRANDFATHER: See those two gravestones? Off in the corner? Those are for Elmer and Buck. They were our guides. Hired by my father.

EDDIE: Old S S?

GRANDFATHER: Old S S hired Elmer and Buck. They were a special breed, those Adirondack guides. They built our camp. made our boats, made our furniture, taught me about the woods. Once my father said, "What do you plan to do with your life? Do you want to go into business? Do you want to learn a profession?" And I said I just wanted to stay at Big Rock and work in the woods with Elmer and Buck.

EDDIE: *(To audience)* We sat for a while, just looking at those gravestones. *(To GRANDFATHER)* Are you all right, Gramp?

GRANDFATHER: I'm fine. *(Blows his nose)* On to Big Rock… Once, when Elmer and I were digging the foundation for the boathouse, I found two Indian arrowheads. Which made me realize that long before Old S S, long before Elmer and Buck, the Indians were up here, catching Big Rock trout.

EDDIE: *(To audience)* We parked at the landing. The caretaker left a boat so we could row over to our camp. After he cooked supper, Gramp showed me how to work the kerosene lamps.

GRANDFATHER: Do you want a light by your bed?

EDDIE: I do, Gramp. It's sort of scary upstairs.

GRANDFATHER: Take it, then. I'll blow it out when I come up.

EDDIE: Don't you want a light down here?

GRANDFATHER: No. I'll just sit and look at the lake.

EDDIE: *(To audience)* And I heard him making a drink in the dark…. And in the morning…

GRANDFATHER: All right, Eddie, up and at 'em.

EDDIE: What are you doing to those hooks, Gramp?

GRANDFATHER: Clipping off the barbs, so it's a fair fight… Now hop in the canoe. I'll do the paddling, you do the casting…. Gently…don't be a water-slapper… Lay it quietly over by that lily pod… Now raise the tip of your rod. Slowly, slowly… There! See? A strike!…Good! You've hooked him… Keep the line taut now… Ease him alongside the boat so I can net him… That's it, that's it!

EDDIE: *(To audience)* And he taught me how to clean them and cook them for breakfast…

GRANDFATHER: Leave the heads and tails on.

EDDIE: Why?

GRANDFATHER: So we'll remember that what we're eating was once beautiful and alive… And don't put so much butter in the pan. Big Rock trout have a taste like nothing else in the world, and you don't want to ruin it….

EDDIE: *(To audience)* Twice at night we went out jacking deer….

GRANDFATHER: Sit here in the stern, between my knees… Ssshhh…quiet…

EDDIE: *(Whispering)* Gramp used a jacking paddle which he carved out of ash-wood when he was just my age…

GRANDFATHER: *(Whispering)* Hear that? That's a deer drinking…. Now I'll shine my light and there! See? …A three-point buck!

EDDIE: Could you shoot him?

GRANDFATHER: At night? With a light? Wouldn't be sporty… Now look at the sky. Let's learn our constellations…

EDDIE: *(To audience)* And we went camping overnight, and Gramp showed me how to do a front flip off a rock, and one night, we just read books by the fire.

GRANDFATHER: Look at this old Atlas, Eddie. Read what it says about Buffalo.

EDDIE: *(Reading)* "Queen City of the Great Lakes…located at the the mouth of the Niagara River…. Named after a Seneca Chief named Buffalo, or possibly for the bison herds who originally roamed the area." *(To GRANDFATHER)* I thought Buffalo came from the French. Beau Fleuve, beautiful river.

GRANDFATHER: Where'd you get that?

EDDIE: Gram said it, actually.

GRANDFATHER: Some people like to gussy things up. Read on.

EDDIE: *(Reading)* "… A teeming, muscular metropolis, with a rough past and a ready future. Sixth largest city in the United States." *(To GRANDFATHER)* Our teacher said we're only thirteenth.

GRANDFATHER: That's because we're being passed by.

EDDIE: Why?

GRANDFATHER: Some say the railroads took over from the canal, and went on to Chicago. Some say our weather is inhospitable. Whatever the reason, we've lost our usefulness.

EDDIE: Can we get it back?

GRANDFATHER: People are trying. But sometimes the world just passes you by. It's a law of life.

EDDIE: What's that noise, Gramp?

GRANDFATHER: That's just a beaver, smacking his tail.

EDDIE: You're sure it isn't a bear?

GRANDFATHER: Oh no. The bears are passing us by, too. Things are getting too fancy for them. I hear the Albrights are putting in a pump.

EDDIE: *(To audience)* Our last day at Big Rock it rained….

GRANDFATHER: If you'll excuse me, Eddie, I'll row over to the landing and hear the news from Europe on the car radio.

EDDIE: *(To audience)* So I found an old snapshot album and looked at pictures of the old days. And guess what? I found a picture of four people, out in the sun, on the front steps of our camp. There was my Grandmother, looking young and pretty, smiling and hugging her knees. Next to her was Gramp, with his arm around her. Standing behind, with his hand on Gramp's shoulder, was Uncle Roger, looking handsome I have to admit. And next to him was this grumpy lady who I guess was Uncle Roger's first wife.

GRANDFATHER: I'm back. What are you doing?

EDDIE: Just looking at old pictures, Gramp.

GRANDFATHER: Let's break camp.

EDDIE: How was the news?

GRANDFATHER: Bad. And getting worse.

EDDIE: Do you think Hitler is insatiable?

GRANDFATHER: Do I think what?

EDDIE: My teacher thinks Hitler has an insatiable appetite for further conquests.

GRANDFATHER: Your teacher may be right.

EDDIE: *(To audience)* The closer we got to Buffalo, the less Gramp talked. And we only stopped once. For a vanilla milkshake.

GRANDFATHER: *(As if ordering)* For the boy. An Old Fashioned for me.

EDDIE: *(To audience)* And that fall, back at school, our first assignment was to write a free composition. So I wrote about my trip to Big Rock. I got a ninety-three on it. My spelling wasn't so hot, but my teacher said I expressed real feeling for my Grandfather.

***

JANE: Look at that, gang! Your grandmother's had something painted on her mailbox. *(To HARVEY)* Slow down, after you turn in, so we can read it.

HARVEY: *(Reading)* "Windover Farm."

JANE: We're getting mighty fancy in our old age…"Windover Farm" indeed.

EDDIE: There's not much wind and it's not a farm.

JANE: You said it, Eddie. And look! They've tacked on a whole new facade! White pillars and everything! Roger certainly is putting his stamp on things. And, oh no! They've put one of those little cast-iron Negro jockeys right by the front door.

EDDIE: Are we supposed to hitch our car to it?

JANE: Exactly, Eddie.

HARVEY: Everything looks very inviting.

JANE: Welcome to Tara, gang.

HARVEY: The Woodriches have a lot of money and know how to spend it.

JANE: Oh I hate these Sundays! I loathe them! I feel like a traitor to Father whenever we're here.

HARVEY: Sssshh. Here she comes.

GRANDMOTHER: Hello, hello, dearies… Run and say hello to your Uncle Roger, children…

JANE: Who's coming today, Mother?

GRANDMOTHER: We'll be eighteen, actually. All of you, of course, and your brother's bringing his new girl. And Roger's asked *his* children and grandchildren. So we've set up a children's table in the hall… Have you all said hello to your Uncle Roger, children? …Good. Then let me show you the croquet things while the grown-ups have cocktails.

JANE: *(To* HARVEY*)* Here goes another Sunday.

HARVEY: Make the most of it, sweetie.

JANE: Anna Karenina at least had the good sense to get out of town.

EDDIE: Who's Anna Karenina?

HARVEY: I thought you were playing croquet.

EDDIE: Gram asked me to wait here. Who's Anna Karenina?

HARVEY: You'll read about her when we send you away to school.

GRANDMOTHER: Now, Eddie. Your Uncle Roger would like to speak to you in the library.

EDDIE: Me?

GRANDMOTHER: Scoot, dearie. He gets impatient.

(The actor playing GRANDFATHER *now plays* UNCLE ROGER. *He might put glasses on.)*

ROGER: Sit down, Eddie.

EDDIE: I swear I didn't do it, Uncle Roger.

ROGER: Do what?

EDDIE: Break the tennis court net. I know who broke it, but I won't squeal. *(To audience)* His own granddaughter broke it, Margie Woodrich. She leaned on it last week, right after I told her not to.

ROGER: I don't want to talk about tennis, Eddie.

EDDIE: Neither do I.

ROGER: I want to talk about your grandfather. I hear you wrote a composition about him for school.

EDDIE: I got a ninety-three on it.

ROGER: May I see it some time?

EDDIE: It's just about fishing at Big Rock.

ROGER: I've been up there, actually.

EDDIE: I saw your picture in the album.

ROGER: I was a good friend of your grandfather's.

EDDIE: You won that silver cup together.

ROGER: Your grandfather's a beautiful athlete. He's good at everything he does.

EDDIE: He doesn't play sports any more. He's resigned from everything except the Saturn Club.

ROGER: I've resigned even from that. We're both exiles these days.

EDDIE: You're both what?

ROGER: Exiles. Cut off. Banished into outer darkness.

EDDIE: Why?

ROGER: Me, because I broke the rules. I can't speak for your grandfather.

EDDIE: Can I go now?

ROGER: I hear you think I stole your grandmother from your grandfather.

EDDIE: Who told you that?

ROGER: My granddaughter. Margie.

EDDIE: *(To audience)* That's the one who broke the net. *(To ROGER)* I just meant…I just said…I just—

ROGER: That's what you told her.

EDDIE: *(To audience; imitating the radio program)* I can see the Shadow will have to pay a call on Margie Woodrich.

ROGER: Let me tell you something, Eddie. I have known and liked both your grandparents for a long time. We grew up together, here in Buffalo. When I became… involved with your grandmother, it changed things. It always does. But I never would have married her, Eddie, if I didn't have great respect for your grandfather. Do you see? Your grandfather is a distinguished man, from a distinguished Buffalo family. Once I was involved with his wife, I had to marry her. Do you understand what I'm saying?

EDDIE: Yes sir. *(To audience)* But I really didn't.

ROGER: Now go play croquet. We'll never mention this again.

EDDIE: O K. *(To audience)* So I got into the croquet game, and whispered to Margie that if she ever squealed on me again, I was going to send her ball all the way into the poison ivy. Which made her cry, because she was two years younger than me.

***

JANE: *(To HARVEY)* That so-called children's table is Father's, you know.

EDDIE: Nancy sat next to the window coming out.

HARVEY: Be quiet, kids. Your mother's trying to talk, and I'm trying to listen, and drive a car at the same time.

JANE: I recognized that table immediately. Old E G had it down at the bank. Then it migrated to the Sun Room at Cooperstown with old S S. Father inherited it, and kept it in the front hall on Summer Street.

HARVEY: How could you possibly tell? All I noticed was a white tablecloth spattered with mashed peas and spilled gravy.

JANE: I looked at the legs. It has lovely old legs.

EDDIE: Who has lovely old legs?

HARVEY: Your grandmother does. Now be quiet.

JANE: He sends her a bill, you know.

HARVEY: What?

JANE: Roger sends Mother a bill for these Sunday lunches.

HARVEY: He sends his own wife a bill?

JANE: All right, *gives*. Gives her a bill. She told me. It's part of the pre-nuptial agreement. Every month he gives her an itemized statement covering food plus maids. Mother writes him a check. When his own family is there, he deducts their costs on a per capita basis.

HARVEY: The Woodriches have always been good about money.

JANE: It's Father's money! He gave her a huge settlement.

HARVEY: At least she's spending it on her family.

JANE: While poor Father sits around, all alone in that cold, dark house.

HARVEY: Where's his resiliency? Where's his old bounce? I never thought I'd be saying this, Jane, but maybe it boils down to the problem of inherited money.

JANE: Explain that, please.

HARVEY: Ever since old E G, no one in your family has worked.

JANE: Father works. He has his own coal business.

HARVEY: Old S S handed him that on a silver platter. It's all been too easy for him. He doesn't want anything.

JANE: He wants Mother.

HARVEY: Well he's lost her, and he's got to move on. Oh look, I detest Roosevelt, but he may be right when he calls for larger inheritance taxes.

JANE: You inherited money.

HARVEY: Just enough to make me want more.

***

GRANDMOTHER: Eddie, do you like flowers?

EDDIE: Not much.

GRANDMOTHER: Some day you will. Some day they'll bring peace into your life. So come have a look at my cutting garden.

EDDIE: O K. O K.

GRANDMOTHER: These will be peonies…great big globes of white and pink….

EDDIE: Goody-goody.

GRANDMOTHER: I have the feeling you're mad at me, Eddie. You've been grumpy ever since you got out here.

EDDIE: How come you didn't take me to lunch last week?

GRANDMOTHER: Lunch?

EDDIE: It was spring vacation. I was just sitting around. You took Nancy to lunch, but you didn't take me.

GRANDMOTHER: I would have, Eddie, but the Garret Club is for women only.

EDDIE: We could have gone somewhere else. We could have gone to Meyer's Grill and had hot roast beef sandwiches.

GRANDMOTHER: I have to go to the Garret Club, dearie. Every Wednesday, rain or shine.

EDDIE: Is the Garret Club a club where they make you go?

GRANDMOTHER: Oh mercy no. In fact, they asked me to resign. But I won't do it, Eddie. They'll have to throw me out the window… Now these will be delphinium if they survive our Buffalo winters.

EDDIE: Do they have hot roast beef sandwiches at the Garret Club?

GRANDMOTHER: They do not. They have creamed chicken, with a small salad on the side.

EDDIE: Then why do you have to go there?

GRANDMOTHER: Because I have to run the gauntlet.

EDDIE: Run the what?

GRANDMOTHER: The gauntlet, Eddie. A gauntlet is when you're captured by Indians, and they make you run through a double line, and everyone takes a swipe at you.

EDDIE: Does everyone take a swipe at you at the Garret Club?

GRANDMOTHER: They do, Eddie. Oh not literally. But it's a big dining room, and my table's way at the other end, and everyone gives me the cold shoulder as I walk by.

EDDIE: Because of Gramp?

GRANDMOTHER: He was a very popular man.

EDDIE: I'd resign from that club, Gram.

GRANDMOTHER: Oh no. Never! Because if you run the gauntlet, and survive, sometimes Indians let you into their tribe.

EDDIE: Do you want be in that tribe?

GRANDMOTHER: Everyone has to have a tribe, Eddie. It gets pretty lonely without one.

EDDIE: Gram…

GRANDMOTHER: What, dearie?

EDDIE: Will you have lunch with Gramp some time?

GRANDMOTHER: No.

EDDIE: Just lunch.

GRANDMOTHER: No.

EDDIE: Not at the Garret Club. At Meyer's Roast Beef, or some place.

GRANDMOTHER: No, dearie. No.

EDDIE: Mom's worried because he never eats lunch.

GRANDMOTHER: One thing about running the gauntlet, Eddie. You can't look back. If you look over your shoulder, you're dead. That much I know… Now let me show you where I'm planning to put the petunias.

***

HARVEY: *(To* JANE*)* Darling, did you hear? Old Mrs Sidway died.

JANE: When?

HARVEY: Last night, apparently. Comfortably. In her apartment.

JANE: I loved old Mrs Sidway.

HARVEY: So did we all.

JANE: I love her apartment.

HARVEY: That's my point.

JANE: It's so light and airy.

HARVEY: Rita Danforth has already made a bid.

JANE: I'll get Father to make a better one.

HARVEY: If he will.

JANE: He will for me. If we can just get him out of that barn of a house, maybe he'll get a new lease on life.

EDDIE: *(To audience)* Mrs Driscoll cooked for Gramp after he moved into his new apartment, but she got lonely and went to Milwaukee to live with her niece. Annie went to live with the nuns. William McKaye died. My mother got a maid named Inez to come to Gramp's during the day, but she was bossy and mean to us children. *(To* JANE*)* And mean even to Gramp!

JANE: I know, Eddie. But it's harder and harder to get people. And we can't just leave him alone.

EDDIE: *(To audience)* And guess what? Gramp's old house was snapped up by Doctor Taubman, who is our dentist. He moved upstairs, and turned the downstairs into offices. It's a strange feeling to go into the old dining room, and have Miss Bacon poke around for cavities, rather than Annie coming in with a plate of Mrs Driscoll's sugar cookies. Of course, maybe the cookies caused the cavities in the first place.

***

HARVEY: *(To* JANE*)* Where've you been, darling? We're all famished, and Mabel in the kitchen is restless and disagreeable.

JANE: I've been to the hospital, that's all.

HARVEY: The hospital?

JANE: Mother had a fall. Off that stupid horse. She was taking some jump, and the horse balked, and over she went. She's broken her leg in three places.

HARVEY: I'm very sorry to hear that.

JANE: I could have predicted it. She's too old to ride. Certainly to jump. Let's hope she's learned her lesson.

EDDIE: What lesson?

HARVEY: I don't believe you were part of this conversation, Eddie.

JANE: The lesson is, Eddie, grow old gracefully. Don't climb on a horse, and canter frantically after some man. Here endeth the lesson.

HARVEY: I imagine Roger will continue to ride.

JANE: Oh yes. Oh yes. He sat by Mother's bedside and blithely announced that he plans to ride this Saturday.

HARVEY: Nobody will ride much longer if Hitler continues to misbehave.

JANE: I hear Roger is misbehaving, too.

EDDIE: Is Uncle Roger insatiable?

HARVEY: None of that, please.

JANE: Apparently he is, Eddie.

HARVEY: (To JANE) I'll send your mother flowers immediately.

EDDIE: Gram loves flowers.

HARVEY: I happen to know that, Eddie.

*****

EDDIE: (To audience) You might think this is all I do—sit around with my parents and worry about my grandparents. Wrong! I have many other interests and activities. Mr Simpson, our new English teacher, asked us to write a free composition on our likes and dislikes. So here's what I wrote… Part One. Things I like. Swimming with my friends in the Saturn Club pool on Saturday mornings, and getting warm in the Steam Room afterwards. Going to the movies at Shea's Elmwood on Saturday afternoons, and making popping noises with our cheeks when the stars kiss at the end. Going to the hockey games at Nichols School on Friday nights and teasing the girls in the bleachers. Diagramming sentences in English class, using colored pencils, so you can see how everything hangs together. Going to Dellhurst Drugstore and reading comic books without having to pay. (Pause) Part Two. Things I don't like. Dancing school, except when we do the Lambeth Walk. Being checked by Doctor Griswald, who feels you up even when it's just a sore throat. Writing all those thank-you notes for Christmas, even though you've just seen the people and said thank you in person. Going to church when there's no skiing. Playing tennis with my father watching because I'll never be as good as he wants me to be. And that's about it. (Pause) When I got my composition back, Mr Simpson wrote the following comments: "You are living a very privileged life, Eddie. With privilege comes responsibility. Some day you and your classmates will be civic leaders in Buffalo. Therefore plan your weekends *constructively*. Visit the Erie County Library and peruse the Mark Twain manuscript. Go to the Albright Art Gallery and contemplate the Greek statuary. Gather your friends around the radio some Saturday afternoon, and listen to the opera from New York. A larger world is beckoning to you. Take advantage of it." *(Pause)* Mr Simpson left during hockey season. He told us he couldn't make a dent in an in-bred school like ours.

***

JANE: *(Calling)* Eddie! Would you come into my room a minute?

EDDIE: What's the trouble?

JANE: Do these look familiar in any way?

EDDIE: What are those?

JANE: These are two valentines, Eddie. Your grandfather got one, your grandmother got the other. Oddly enough they both have the same note at the end.

EDDIE: Do they?

JANE: They both say, "Let's get reconciled."

EDDIE: Oh yeah?

JANE: It's a nice, big word, "reconciled." Do you know what it means?

EDDIE: It means to settle, or resolve, a dispute.

JANE: Do you know how to spell it?

EDDIE: Reconciled. R-E-C-O-N-S-I-L-E-D. Reconciled.

JANE: Strange. That's the way it's spelled in these two valentines.

EDDIE: So?

JANE: So it's misspelled, Eddie.

EDDIE: Oh.

JANE: Did you write these valentines?

EDDIE: You don't have to tell who sends a valentine.

JANE: Don't do it any more, darling. It's a sweet idea, but don't. It just rubs salt on the wounds. O K?

EDDIE: O K.

HARVEY: *(Calling)* I'm home!

JANE: We won't mention this to your father. He'd just get mad.

EDDIE: About the valentines. Or about the misspelling.

JANE: Both, I'm afraid. Now let's go down and have dinner.

HARVEY: I'm late because we were discussing the war in Europe at the Saturn Club Grill.

JANE: Oh the war, the war.

HARVEY: I want everyone at this table to know that the news is bad and getting worse.

EDDIE: The purple's getting larger every year.

HARVEY: The purple, Eddie?

EDDIE: On our homeroom map. Germany and Japan are purple. Mr Kenyon says they're like two great bruises spreading out all over the world.

HARVEY: That is a very apt analogy, Eddie…. Jane, tell Mabel the mashed potatoes are lumpy again.

JANE: Mabel has given notice. She found a job making Bell Aerocobras down at the Falls.

EDDIE: Mabel will be making *Aerocobras*?

HARVEY: Don't shout, Eddie.

EDDIE: But the Aerocrobra is our best fighter plane!

HARVEY: Mabel may make planes, but she can't make mashed potatoes. I'm sure your mother will find someone better.

JANE: I'm not even looking. From here on in, yours truly produces the meals.

HARVEY: You're talking about for the duration?

JANE: I'm talking about forever. I'm tired of organizing my life around some creature in the kitchen.

HARVEY: Darling! You can hardly boil water!

JANE: I can learn, can't I? If I can find time. When I'm not coping with Mother and Father.

HARVEY: I suppose you had lunch with her today at the Garret Club.

JANE: Where else.

HARVEY: Anyone speaking to her yet?

JANE: Not really. And that leg has never healed properly, so it takes her twice as long to navigate the room.

EDDIE: She's running the gauntlet.

JANE: Run? With that leg, she can hardly walk.

HARVEY: A warmer climate would help.

JANE: They tried that, remember? Palm Springs? And Father tried fishing on the Keys. But here they are, back again, all three of them. Oh God, they can't leave! And neither can you and I! Our families have been here too long.

HARVEY: I'm the Johnny-Come-Lately around here. My mother's father came from Troy.

EDDIE: Troy, New York? Or Troy, Asia Minor.

HARVEY: Don't get smart, please, Eddie.

JANE: We're stuck, Eddie. We are stuck! Sometimes it feels as if they've drained the lake, and the river's gone dry, and we're all left flopping around in the mud.

EDDIE: Did you know that trout need a continuous flow of fresh water in order to survive?

HARVEY: We're not talking about trout, Eddie.

JANE: Maybe we are! Where's *our* fresh water? Where's our new blood? We're all turned in on ourselves. We're becoming like—Europeans!

HARVEY: Oh now darling.

JANE: Oh I don't know . All I know is if Mother continues to drag her badge of shame around the Garret Club, and Father continues to drink his life away at the Saturn Club, I think I'll go stark raving mad!

HARVEY: Children: we are going through some very difficult times. The family's in trouble, the city's in trouble, and the world is in the worst trouble of all.

EDDIE: What can we do about it, Pop?

HARVEY: I'll tell you exactly what. Eddie, you can collect tin cans throughout the neighborhood. Nancy, you can knit argyle socks for the Free French. And Tim, you can put less butter on your Hot Cross Bun... Now, Eddie, tell me. What color is Great Britain on that map of yours?

EDDIE: Pink.

HARVEY: The British Empire is pink. Fine. Then we must all pray very hard for the pink.

***

EDDIE: Saturday mornings were when my father played the piano.

HARVEY: *(Singing)* "There may be trouble ahead..."

EDDIE: *(To audience)* He finished his Shredded Wheat, which is made right near Buffalo, and sat right down in his pajamas, and played and sang.

HARVEY: *(Singing)* "But while there's music and moonlight and love and romance..."

EDDIE: *(To audience)* He had all this sheet music on the rack, with Fred Astaire and Ginger Rogers jumping over the moon, and grinning at each other while they were doing it.

HARVEY: *(Singing)* "Let's face the music and dance..." *(To EDDIE)* Every family should have a piano, Eddie. Show me a house without a piano, and I'll show you an unhappy family living inside.

EDDIE: *(To audience)* And Saturday mornings were also when my Mother went up to her bedroom and ordered the weekend groceries over the telephone...

JANE: *(On telephone)* I'd like a loaf of Bond Bread—unsliced, please—and how are your peas today?

HARVEY: *(Singing)* "I'm putting all my eggs in one basket..."

JANE: *(On telephone)* And six loin lambchops... *(Hand over receiver)* Nancy, would you come upstairs a minute, please?

EDDIE: *(To audience)* Sometimes my Mother tried to get Nancy to do the ordering.

JANE: *(Hands over receiver)* Nancy, you've got to learn to use the telephone. It's an important instrument in our lives.

EDDIE: *(To audience)* But Nancy would say "I'm shy."

JANE: *(As if to Nancy)* Nonsense. These are modern times. Every woman has got to learn how to assert herself with tradesmen. Now give it a try.

HARVEY: *(Singing)* "Heaven… I'm in heaven… And the cares that hang around me through the week…"

JANE: *(On telephone)* Mr Rosenblat? I'm putting my daughter Nancy on the phone… What? Oh no! *(As if to Nancy)* He says they're stopping Saturday deliveries. *(Into telephone)* All right, Mr Rosenblat. Nancy and I will drive right down, and you can show us how to pick things out. *(To Nancy)* Maybe we'll learn something, Nancy.

HARVEY: *(To EDDIE)* I wish you hadn't given up piano lessons, Eddie.

EDDIE: I hated those piano lessons.

HARVEY: That's all very well, but some day you'll be sitting idly on a piano bench, and some lovely girl will sit down beside you, and put her cheek next to yours, and say, "Play Gershwin for me. Play Irving Berlin", and you won't be able to do it. It's all very, very sad. *(Sings)* "Isn't it a Lovely Day to be caught in the rain…"

JANE: *(Calling)* Your grandmother wants to speak to you on the telephone, Eddie.

EDDIE: Why?

JANE: Don't ask me. I only live here. Go speak to her, please.

HARVEY: *(Singing)* "Must you dance…every dance…with the same fortunate man?… You have danced with him since the evening began…"

GRANDMOTHER: *(On telephone)* I understand you like the movies, Eddie.

EDDIE: *(On telephone)* I do.

GRANDMOTHER: Let's you and I go to the movies this afternoon. Your Uncle Roger is off riding, so we'll have a big date.

EDDIE: Um…

GRANDMOTHER: Or have you got other plans?

EDDIE: *(To audience)* I did, actually. I was supposed to see James Cagney in *City for Conquest* with my gang from school.

GRANDMOTHER: *(On telephone)* We'll see *Wuthering Heights*. It's my favorite book.

EDDIE: *(Reluctantly)* Sounds great, Gram.

GRANDMOTHER: I'll pick you up in my car at twelve-thirty, and we'll have lunch at *The Quaker Bonnet*. The movie starts at twenty past two.

JANE: Wouldn't you know she'd pick *The Quaker Bonnet*, right in the thick of things.

HARVEY: *(Singing)* "Putting on my Top Hat… Getting out my white tie…"

GRANDMOTHER: Hop in the car, Eddie. And we're off.

EDDIE: Say, Gram. How come you don't use second gear when you drive?

GRANDMOTHER: I suppose I believe in getting right to the point.

EDDIE: Didn't William McKaye teach you to use second?

GRANDMOTHER: Oh William, William McKaye. That dear, dear man.

EDDIE: Do you miss him?

GRANDMOTHER: I miss a lot of things.

EDDIE: That's a red light, Gram.

GRANDMOTHER: So it is, so it is.

EDDIE: See what happens, Gram? When you slow down, the car starts bucking. This would have been an excellent time to shift into second gear.

GRANDMOTHER: *(Laughing)* There are no second gears in American life, Eddie.

EDDIE: I don't get it.

GRANDMOTHER: I was paraphrasing Mr F Scott Fitzgerald, who spent his formative years right here in Buffalo. In fact, I danced with him at dancing school. He was a wonderful dancer. And what he actually said was, "There are no second acts in American life."

EDDIE: He said that at *dancing* school?

GRANDMOTHER: Oh no, dearie. He said it later, when he was very famous.... But here we are at *The Quaker Bonnet*. If I can get this thing to park.

EDDIE: *(To audience)* A couple of my friends were sitting at the counter, spinning on their stools, and shooting straw-wrappers with their straws. And I saw Margie Woodrich— remember? the one who broke the tennis net?—huddling in a booth with the Richmond sisters, peeking at us and giggling.

GRANDMOTHER: Are you embarrassed, having lunch with your own grandmother?

EDDIE: It's better than having lunch with somebody else's.

GRANDMOTHER: Oh Eddie. You are a sketch.... Thank you for that valentine, by the way.

EDDIE: You knew it was me because of the misspelling, right?

GRANDMOTHER: I knew it was you because of the thought. It was a sweet thought. Impossible, but a sweet one.

EDDIE: I keep thinking it.

GRANDMOTHER: I hear you've written another composition. About your grandfather.

EDDIE: I wrote more about Big Rock.

GRANDMOTHER: I used to go there all the time.

EDDIE: I saw your picture in the album. I also saw what you wrote in the guest book.

GRANDMOTHER: Oh dear. What did I write?

EDDIE: You wrote, "rain, rain, rain."

GRANDMOTHER: *(Laughing)* Sounds like I was in a bad mood. *(Pause)* It didn't always rain.

EDDIE: *(To audience)* Then Old Mrs Potter came in, and walked right by our table.

GRANDMOTHER: *(Looking up)* Hello, Alma.

EDDIE: *(To audience)* But Old Mrs Potter walked right on by. Of course, it's hard for older people to put on the brakes once they get up momentum.

GRANDMOTHER: Give me your arm, please, Eddie. And we're off to the movies.

EDDIE: How's your leg, Gram?

GRANDMOTHER: It's perfectly fine when I have a handsome man to lean on.

EDDIE: *(To audience)* Shea's Great Lakes is a beautiful theatre, with a real fountain in the lobby and a huge, high purple ceiling…

GRANDMOTHER: Look. It's starting. Now let's settle down.

(EDDIE *and* GRANDMOTHER *watch the movie.*)

GRANDMOTHER: Oh my… oh my…oh my…

EDDIE: I guess that's the end, Gram.

GRANDMOTHER: *(Wiping her eyes)* Yes… Oh dear… That's that…. Didn't you adore it?

EDDIE: They did a lot of talking.

GRANDMOTHER: But they talked so well! *(Pause)* What did you think of Catharine Earnshaw, Eddie.

EDDIE: Cathy? She was sort of a pill, maybe.

GRANDMOTHER: A pill? A pill?

EDDIE: The way she just dies that way.

GRANDMOTHER: Oh, but don't you see? That was the point. She'd married the wrong man.

EDDIE: Oh.

GRANDMOTHER: He was a perfectly nice man, in fact, he was nicer than Heathcliff, but he was just plain wrong for her.

EDDIE: Oh.

GRANDMOTHER: In those days, when you married someone, you were stuck for life. So her spirit wasted away.

EDDIE: I get it.

GRANDMOTHER: Now if she had run off with Heathcliff, it would have been a very different story. But in those days, you simply couldn't run off with people.

EDDIE: I get it now.

GRANDMOTHER: You had to stick it out. And that killed her.

EDDIE: Is Uncle Roger like Heathcliff to you, Gram?

GRANDMOTHER: Oh, Eddie, aren't you the limit!

EDDIE: He is, isn't he?

GRANDMOTHER: Actually, yes. In some ways. I mean, we grew up together—oh, not in the same *house*, stuck out in the moors, like Cathy and Heathcliff. But here in Buffalo, which, come to think of it, is sort of the same thing… Oh, and listen to this: one winter, when we were older, your grandfather took me for a sleigh-ride around the Meadow, and I remember thinking that the coachman was acting very peculiar. Very peculiar indeed. So I looked at him carefully, and guess who it was?

EDDIE: William McKaye?

GRANDMOTHER: Wrong! It was your Uncle Roger! All bundled up in a muffler and cap. He was playing a joke on us. I mean, there he was, sitting right in the driver's seat, all along!

EDDIE: So finally you ran off with him.

GRANDMOTHER: Yes I did, Eddie. Finally I ran off with him. But we didn't run very far, did we? Not far at all. Maybe not quite far enough.

EDDIE: Gram…

GRANDMOTHER: What?

EDDIE: Do you ever see Gramp now?

GRANDMOTHER: Never.

EDDIE: I mean when you come into town.

GRANDMOTHER: Never.

EDDIE: I mean, at a party or something. Don't you ever just run into him?

GRANDMOTHER: Never. Never. Never.

EDDIE: Do you ever want to?

GRANDMOTHER: Oh Eddie, sometimes I think… But here we are at your front door.

EDDIE: Want to come in and say hello, Gram?

GRANDMOTHER: Better not, Eddie. Uncle Roger gets very upset if I'm not there when he gets back from his riding.

EDDIE: Thank you for a nice time, Gram.

GRANDMOTHER: Some day, Eddie, I'll tell you my story. Some day. I mean it. So you can write a composition all about me.

EDDIE: Goodbye, Gram. *(Calling after her)* And don't forget second gear!

***

JANE: *(Calling out)* Kids! Stop the game and come up to the house, please!

EDDIE: *(To audience)* We were all playing Touch Out at Gram's on Sunday, December 7th, when the Japanese bombed Pearl Harbor.

GRANDMOTHER: Bring your plates into the living room, everybody, and we'll listen to the news on the Capehart.

HARVEY: You children will remember this day for the rest of your lives.

GRANDMOTHER: I'm afraid this means your Uncle Freddy will have to go! And Roger's sons as well.

JANE: Where is he, by the way?

GRANDMOTHER: Roger? Riding, of course.

HARVEY: I hear they're closing down the East Aurora Hunt.

GRANDMOTHER: If they do, he'll have to stay home…I don't know whether that's good or bad.

***

EDDIE: (To audience) That same fall, Gramp started dating Mrs Mitchell.

HARVEY: I'm not sure I like that word "dating", Eddie… (To EDDIE) Your grandfather is *seeing* Mrs Mitchell, Eddie. He is enjoying Mrs Mitchell's company.

JANE: At least, she gets him out and around.

EDDIE: (To JANE) Did you fix them up?

HARVEY: Your mother *introduced* them, Eddie.

JANE: At old Mr Holloway's funeral. They both were sitting in back, and I thought why not? Now let's just keep our fingers crossed.

EDDIE: (To audience) Mrs Mitchell's husband had come to Buffalo to make Curtiss-Wright P-40's, and had a heart attack, and died.

HARVEY: (To JANE) I hear he didn't provide for her as well as he might have. The poor thing was left high and dry.

JANE: (To HARVEY) She was planning to go back to Charleston to live with her daughter. But once she met Father, she decided to stay on.

HARVEY: She realized the warmth and charm of Buffalo.

JANE: She also realized that Father's coal company had been bought for a tidy sum by Ashland Oil.

EDDIE: (To audience) Gramp brought Mrs Mitchell to our house for Christmas Eve. (To JANE) What's Mrs Mitchell's first name?

HARVEY: Mrs Mitchell, to you.

JANE: Her first name happens to be Fanny.

EDDIE: Fanny? FANNY? How come?

JANE: It's short for Frances. Actually, it fits. Or doesn't. Depending on what's she's wearing.

EDDIE: Do we call her Aunt Fanny?

JANE: I wouldn't jump the gun.

HARVEY: Welcome, Fanny! Welcome, Ed! Merry Christmas to all!… Come in and sit down… There's a step here, Fanny. Let me take your arm. I've always believed in a step-down living-room. It gives a party momentum, right from the start…. And here we are: Fanny: a Manhattan for you, and Ed, your usual Old Fashioned.

FANNY: (Played by the actress who plays the GRANDMOTHER; Southern accent) I'm terribly worried about the war. Those beautiful cities in Europe. I wonder if they'll ever be the same.

EDDIE: "The Last Time I saw Paris" was sixth on the Hit Parade.

HARVEY: Eddie, other people are talking.

FANNY: I used to love to travel. The first thing I want to do after the war is go to Europe and visit all the old sights. *(To* GRANDFATHER*)* Wouldn't you love to go to Europe, Edward?

GRANDFATHER: I've been there.

EDDIE: Gramp's been hunting in Africa.

FANNY: I believe I prefer the more temperate zones.

HARVEY: As do I, as do I, Fanny.

FANNY: I'd love to go by boat. I want to dance my way over, and dance my way back, on the *Normandie* or the *Ile de France.*

EDDIE: I'd love to go salmon fishing in Iceland.

HARVEY: Again, Eddie, I'll have to ask you not to interrupt.

GRANDFATHER: How about grouse shooting in Scotland, Eddie?

EDDIE: I'd love that, too, Gramp.

HARVEY: There are only two ways to travel, Fanny. First class. Or with children. I fear I prefer the former.

FANNY: I couldn't agree with you more.

GRANDFATHER: Who lit that fire?

HARVEY: I believe I did, Ed.

GRANDFATHER: That is one poor excuse for a fire.

FANNY: I think it's a lovely fire.

HARVEY: Thank you, Fanny.

EDDIE: What's wrong with the fire, Gramp?

GRANDFATHER: If you'll wait a minute, I'll show you.

HARVEY: That fire is perfectly fine. *(To FANNY)* You should know a man seven years, Fanny, before you fuss with his fire.

FANNY: Oh yes! We say that in the South.

GRANDFATHER: I've known you much longer than that, Harvey, and you still can't build a decent fire.

HARVEY: You'll notice, Fanny, that in Buffalo, we don't use kindling. Every fireplace has a built-in gas jet. That's because we sit on large deposits of natural gas.

GRANDFATHER: *(Sardonically)* That's true enough.

HARVEY: A fire is simply a question of lighting a match.

GRANDFATHER: A good fire is more than that.

JANE: Soup's on, everybody… And guess what, Father? I found a bottle of wine which came from Old S S's cellar in Cooperstown.

FANNY: No wine for Edward, please.

GRANDFATHER: What's that?

FANNY: You're trying to cut down, Edward.

GRANDFATHER: Am I?

HARVEY: Take my arm, Fanny. We'll try to do justice to the groaning board.

FANNY: I'd be de-lighted.

GRANDFATHER: Eddie, stay here and see how I remake this fire.

EDDIE: What do you do, Gramp?

GRANDFATHER: To begin with, I use three logs. Always use three. Put the largest one in back. There. See? That fire will now burn quietly all during dinner, and be waiting for us when we come back. Sometime I'll show you how to bank a fire so that it lasts all night.

JANE: Father! Come carve, please! Harvey can't seem to locate the second joint.

GRANDFATHER: Be right there. *(Low, to* EDDIE*)* Eddie, throw a generous splash of whiskey into this glass… Thank you… Now let's go in and face the music.

EDDIE: *(To audience)* After dinner, we sang songs around the piano.

JANE, HARVEY & FANNY: "Bring the torch, Jeanette, Isabella… Bring the torch, to the stable run…"

HARVEY: *(To* GRANDFATHER*)* Come join us, Ed.

GRANDFATHER: I think I might make myself a highball.

FANNY: Yoo hoo! Edward! I wouldn't.

GRANDFATHER: You wouldn't. I would.

JANE & HARVEY: *(Continuing singing)* "It is Christmas, good folk of the village…"

FANNY: Seriously, Edward. We're almost ready to go.

GRANDFATHER: Are we?

FANNY: *I'm* ready, then.

GRANDFATHER: I'm not.

*(*JANE *and* HARVEY *stop singing.)*

FANNY: When do you think you might be?

GRANDFATHER: I don't know.

(Pause)

FANNY: I wonder if someone would mind calling me a taxi.

EDDIE: *(To audience)* I wanted to say "You're a taxi, Mrs Mitchell."

HARVEY: I'd be delighted to take you home, Fanny.

FANNY: I am glad there are *some* gentlemen left in this war-torn world.

JANE: Oh Fanny, won't you stay?

FANNY: Not when I'm not wanted… Where's my coat, please? Where are my galoshes? … Ah here they are.

EDDIE: *(To audience)* When she bent over to put on her galoshes, I could see why they called her Fanny.

FANNY: Goodnight, Jane… Goodnight, children… I appreciate your help, Harvey.

HARVEY: We're off, then… Back in two shakes of a lamb's tail.

(Pause)

JANE: Oh, Father.

GRANDFATHER: She's not your mother.

JANE: Why don't you children start on the dishes, please?

EDDIE: My turn to dry. *(To audience)* But whenever the water wasn't running, we could hear my mother talking…

JANE: *(Pleadingly)* Oh Father, don't… Oh Father, stop . You've really got to move on, Father. Please….

***

EDDIE: *(To audience)* That spring, my Uncle Freddy joined the Royal Canadian Air Force. He tried the Army Air Corps first, but they wouldn't let him in.

JANE: *(To EDDIE)* Because of his asthma. The poor thing's had asthma all his life.

HARVEY: He did a very brave thing, Eddie. He drove straight up to Toronto, swallowed some pill which helps him breathe, and the Canadians took him on the spot.

JANE: So now he'll marry Teresa before they ship him overseas.

EDDIE: *(To audience)* Teresa's his girl. Teresa Dugan.

HARVEY: *(To EDDIE)* Teresa is a very lovely woman.

EDDIE: *(To audience)* Teresa's a Catholic.

HARVEY: *(To EDDIE)* I don't think we need to get into all that.

JANE: *(To HARVEY)* We *have* to get into all that. The Bishop won't let them get married in the Cathedral.

HARVEY: What?

JANE: He'll only let them have the Annex. And they can't have organ music.

HARVEY: Why not?

JANE: Because even that would make it too official. He proposed we use some woman who plays the harp.

HARVEY: A harp? At a wedding?

JANE: And Freddy has to sign a paper saying their children will be Catholic for the rest of their lives.

EDDIE: Even if they don't want to be?

JANE: The Bishop says that's the deal. Take it or leave it.

HARVEY: The Catholics think they've cornered the market on religion, Eddie. It can be extremely irritating.

JANE: Irritating? It's infuriating.

HARVEY: Of course we have our own ceremonies, too. I'll reserve the Saturn Club for a large cocktail party, and not invite the Bishop.

***

EDDIE: *(To audience)* That spring my Grandmother gave a going-away lunch for Uncle Freddy and Teresa.

JANE: *(To* EDDIE*)* And for Uncle Roger's sons, too. One is going into the Marines and the other the Navy.

EDDIE: How come I have to sit at the children's table, and Nancy doesn't?

HARVEY: Because Nancy's older.

EDDIE: So I have to sit and watch those Woodrich kids flip peas with their spoons and splash each other from their fingerbowls?

HARVEY: Why don't you have a quiet conversation with little Margie Woodrich? I hear you asked her to the Middle School dance.

EDDIE: Cut it out, Pop.

JANE: Yes, Harvey. Don't tease.

GRANDMOTHER: Welcome! Welcome all! …Say hello to Uncle Roger, children.

HARVEY: May I have everyone's attention, please? …Will everyone please stop talking for one minute?… Let those who have ears, let them hear, please…

(Everyone settles down.)

HARVEY: Thank you… I believe I am the Prince Consort in this family, and as such, I feel obliged to say that this is a lovely luncheon, Madeleine.

GRANDMOTHER: Thank you, Harvey.

HARVEY: The roast of beef is as rare as a day in June, the Yorkshire pudding light as a feather, and the asparagus on toast unparalled.

GRANDMOTHER: I'll tell Jo-Ann.

HARVEY: I'll go out and tell her myself, as soon as we finish this superb feast. I fear with meat rationing coming in, we won't enjoy its likes again for the duration.

ROGER: What's for dessert?

GRANDMOTHER: A surprise, Roger. Be patient.

HARVEY: Meanwhile, I want to say a few words to my brother-in-law, as well as to my step-brothers-in-law, before they all march off to war. We all know what Richard Lovelace wrote under similar circumstances…

ROGER: We all *don't* know, Harvey. But I'm sure you'll tell us.

HARVEY: I'd be glad to, Roger. *(Reciting)*
"True a new mistress now I chase,
The first foe in the field,
And with a stronger faith embrace,
A sword, a horse, a shield.
Yet this inconstancy is such
As you too shall adore;
I could not love thee, dear, so much,
Loved I not honor more."

OTHERS: Bravo… Hear, hear… Well done, Harvey.

GRANDMOTHER: May I add something to that, please?

HARVEY: Certainly, Madeleine… Let me help you to your feet.

GRANDMOTHER: I hate to speak in public, but I simply must say that I feel very lucky to have such a wonderful family. First, my dear children… *(Softly, aside)* You can begin clearing the salad plates, Eunice… *(To the group again)* And my thoughtful step-sons…and my very lively grandchildren and step-grandchildren, over there at the children's table… *(Calling off)* Don't stand on that chair, lovey! That's a valuable antique! Eddie! Keep an eye on the little ones, please! *(To the group again)* And of course when I say my family, I include everyone's husband, or wife, or fiancée.

ROGER: Do you include me?

GRANDMOTHER: Of course I do, dear. These Sundays are my life.

ROGER: Bring on the dessert.

GRANDMOTHER: Now hold your horses, Roger. I'm not quite finished. *(Aside)* Don't forget to clean off the crumbs, Eunice. Thank you. *(To others again)* I want to say something else to my family. *(Pause)* I want to say thank you. For sticking by me. Through thick and through thin. At first, I was afraid some of you might not come out here. I mean, there are still people in town who… But I mean, here you all are, aren't you? Here you all are! You've forgiven me, and life has gone on, and that makes me very, very happy.

ROGER: Time to sit down, Madeleine.

GRANDMOTHER: Yes, I will. I plan to. Look at me, standing up here, talking about myself. When I should be talking about you dear boys going off to war. Oh, if I could take your place, boys, I'd go in a minute. Because you're just beginning your lives, and I've had mine, haven't I? I've had more than my share. I've had two lives, really. I've had two wonderful families. And I've been married to two of the most attractive men in Buffalo. How many women in the world can—

ROGER: That's enough, Madeleine. Sit down.

GRANDMOTHER: I will. But I also have to say…

JANE: Look, Mother. Here comes the dessert!

ALL: Oh… Ah… Yummy.

ROGER: What is that thing? Jello?

GRANDMOTHER: That is Floating Island, Roger. Jo-Ann made it specially for Freddy.

ROGER: Never heard of it.

GRANDMOTHER: We used to have it all the time on Summer Street, didn't we, Freddy? Didn't we, Jane? Remember Annie bringing out Mrs Driscoll's Floating Island?

ROGER: Any chocolate cake out there?

GRANDMOTHER: Oh now be nice, Roger. Poor Jo-Ann worked very hard on this Floating Island. She also managed to find some mint for the iced tea, and you'll notice she even made butter-balls. *(Calls over)* Have you ever made butterballs, children? We'll do it together some time. Just for fun. What you do is take two wooden paddles and dip them in ice-water and—

ROGER: You've had too much wine, Madeleine.

HARVEY: Hold on there, Roger.

ROGER: Woman stands up, and won't sit down.

HARVEY: Never mind now.

GRANDMOTHER: No, he's right, Harvey. I've been talking too much. I'm sitting, I'm sitting.

HARVEY: Let me help you, Madeleine.

GRANDMOTHER: Thank you, Harvey… There. See, Roger? I've sat.

ROGER: You talk too much, Madeleine.

HARVEY: You can talk as long as you like, Madeleine.

ROGER: Says who?

HARVEY: I say so, Roger, my friend.

ROGER: This is my house. This is my table.

EDDIE: *(To audience; low)* This was Gramp's house. That was Gramp's table.

HARVEY: Roger, my good friend, I really cannot allow—

ROGER: You can't allow? I do the allowing around here.

HARVEY: I'm sorry, Roger, but when a woman is addressed in that manner, I have to intervene.

ROGER: Want to step outside and do your intervening there, Harvey? Want to do that?

GRANDMOTHER: No, now stop, both of you! Look. I'm finished. I'm done. I'll be as quiet as a mouse.

ROGER: Tell Jo-Ann I'll be in the library, Madeleine. And tell her to bring me a god-damn piece of chocolate cake!

GRANDMOTHER: Oh dear… Oh dear…

HARVEY: I'll go bring him back into the fold.

GRANDMOTHER: NO DON'T! Don't, Harvey! It will just make things worse.

HARVEY: It's the war, of course. This stupid war. Wars do that to people. They make everyone misbehave.

GRANDMOTHER: Oh yes. That must be it. The war.

EDDIE: *(To audience)* After lunch, a professional photographer came to take pictures of my grandmother and Uncle Freddy and Teresa, standing in the doorway with an American flag behind them. Gram hid her cane behind one of the columns. We all clapped when he took the picture.

GRANDMOTHER: *(To* EDDIE*)* Now Eddie, dear, go knock quietly on the door of the library, and tell your Uncle Roger that it's his turn. With *his* children. *(To others)* Roger should have a picture, too.

EDDIE: *(To audience)* So I knocked on his door, but… *(To* GRANDMOTHER*)* He said he was busy, Gram. He wouldn't even open the door.

GRANDMOTHER: Oh.

JANE: Maybe it's time we got going.

GRANDMOTHER: That might be best.

***

EDDIE: *(To audience)* Remember this girl Margie Woodrich? I used to think she was a brat but then she improved. That's why I asked her to the Middle School dance. But guess who had to drive us? My father.

HARVEY: I see you're following in the family footsteps.

EDDIE: Meaning what?

HARVEY: Falling in love with a Woodrich.

EDDIE: Jesus. Stop teasing.

HARVEY: I will if you stop saying Jesus.

EDDIE: I was already nervous about being in a car with my father and a girl at the same time. And he wasn't helping.

HARVEY: What've you got in that box?

EDDIE: What box?

HARVEY: That box, Eddie. In your lap.

EDDIE: Oh this. This is a war-sage.

HARVEY: A what?

EDDIE: War-sage. Like a corsage. Only different.

HARVEY: Explain, please.

EDDIE: *(Patiently)* They put defense stamps on little green stems so they look like flowers, and bunch them together, like a corsage. So they call it a war-sage. Get it?

HARVEY: She might prefer a gardenia.

EDDIE: This helps the war effort. *(To audience)* We were getting closer to where she lived. And I was getting even more nervous. *(To* HARVEY*)* Pop. Will you tell me something without teasing?…

HARVEY: Ask away.

EDDIE: How do you make conversation with a girl?

HARVEY: That's easy. First, you break the ice.

EDDIE: Break the ice?

HARVEY: Look her right in the eye, and say, "You fascinate me."

EDDIE: Pop…

HARVEY: Try it. Then get more personal. Tell her she has lovely shoulders. With Margie, you might mention her nose.

EDDIE: Come on, Pop…

HARVEY: The Woodriches have distinguished noses. Compliment Margie on hers.

EDDIE: I can't do that, Pop.

HARVEY: Of course you can. And after that, simply ask her the oldest question in the world.

EDDIE: What's that?

HARVEY: Just say, "What have you been doing lately?" The stupidest woman in Buffalo will rise to the bait.

EDDIE: What if she gets boring?

HARVEY: She won't be, if she's attractive.

EDDIE: You're teasing again.

HARVEY: Try it and see… And here we are at the Woodrich house.

EDDIE: *(To audience)* She sat between us in front, and put the war-sage in her lap.

HARVEY: Did Eddie show you your war-sage, Margie?

EDDIE: She said she loved it. But when he dropped us off, she said she wouldn't wear it. *(As if to Margie)* Why not? It never wilts. And when you get home, you can take off the stamps, and put them in your stamp book, and eventually purchase a twenty-five dollar war bond. *(To audience)* She said it smelled like glue. *(As if to Margie)* It cost three dollars more than a gardenia! *(To audience)* She said money wasn't everything. But then the music started so we had to dance. And soon there was a quiet song so we had to talk. I figured I'd try what my father told me. *(As if to Margie)* You fascinate me, by the way. *(To audience)* She said, "What?" *(To Margie)* You've got a great nose. *(To audience)* She said, "knock it off." *(To Margie)* O K, then. What have you been doing lately? *(To audience)* This made her start yacking away, but the music got loud, so I had to bend down my head to hear. And know what? It felt kind of neat when her lips touched my ear, so what she said didn't make much difference. Which means my father was right—for once in his life.

***

JANE: No wonder Martin Luther got fed up.

HARVEY: What's the matter?

JANE: The Catholics. Freddy's wedding will be a pseudo-ceremony in a pseudo-church with pseudo-music. We might as well order fake flowers.

HARVEY: She could order war-sages, right, Eddie?

EDDIE: Cut it out, Dad, please.

JANE: No wonder this city is falling apart! We're all eyeing each other across these silly boundaries! The Irish make up these dumb rules, the Poles won't contribute a dime to the Philharmonic, and the Jews run off to New York. And we're just as bad.

HARVEY: I like to think our group is a little more open-minded, thank you.

JANE: Tell them that at the Saturn Club. Which just black-balled Jack Levy.

HARVEY: At least the Dugans can give the reception there.

JANE: As our guests. Period.

EDDIE: May I ask a question?

HARVEY: If you have to.

EDDIE: Are Gramp and Gram both coming to the wedding?

HARVEY: Of course they are. They're the parents of the groom.

EDDIE: What about Uncle Roger?

JANE: He's escorting your grandmother.

EDDIE: You mean, they'll all be there *together*?

JANE: We've worked it all out, Eddie.

EDDIE: But they haven't seen each other since she ran off.

JANE: Your grandmother and Uncle Roger will arrive early and sit in front. Your grandfather will show up later and stay in back.

EDDIE: Can I sit with him?

JANE: Good idea, Eddie. Then after the service, you can drive with him straight to the Saturn Club where we'll whisk him through the receiving line. He'll have one glass of champagne, and be out the door, before Mother and Roger even arrive.

HARVEY: One glass? Your father? One?

JANE: He's agreed, Harvey. All he wants to do is kiss Teresa and shake Freddy's hand.

EDDIE: What if Gram and Uncle Roger are there, too?

JANE: They won't be. After the ceremony, I've got them to go over to the Dugans to look at the wedding presents, which will take at least half an hour..

HARVEY: Your mother is a better organizer than Field Marshall Montgomery.

EDDIE: *(To audience)* So the wedding day arrived. *(To* JANE*)* There's Gramp.

JANE: Where?… Oh no. He's early. Take him to his seat, Eddie. Try to distract him.

EDDIE: Hi, Gramp. Take my arm. I'll usher you.

GRANDFATHER: Suppose I just navigate under my own steam.

EDDIE: *(To audience)* He walked very carefully. I think he might have had a couple of Old Fashioneds. *(To* GRANDFATHER*)* Sit here, Gramp.

GRANDFATHER: I see they want to put me in the back of the bus.

EDDIE: *(To audience)* At weddings, you're supposed to face front, and look at the flowers. But Gramp kept turning around and watching the door. And soon in came Gram, using her cane, and wearing a big hat. Uncle Roger was with her. Gramp stared so hard that other people stared at *him*. Then an usher showed up, so Gram took his arm, and limped up the aisle, with Uncle Roger behind. And Gramp watched them all the way. Then the harp lady started twanging *Here Comes the Bride*, and the bridesmaids started sliding up the aisle, and then Teresa, with a veil and a long train behind. But my grandfather didn't care about that. He just kept staring at my grandmother all during the ceremony *(To* GRANDFATHER*)* That's all, Gramp. We should go to the reception now, to get ahead of the crowd. *(To audience)* But he wouldn't move. I knew he was waiting for Gram to come back down the aisle. Which she finally did, hanging on the arm of an usher, trying not to look too gimpy, with Uncle Roger bringing up the rear. I think she sensed where Gramp was sitting because she kept shooting these quick little glances toward him. When she passed by, I thought I heard him give a quiet groan, like a dog does when it lies down. *(To* GRANDFATHER*)* Time to go now, Gramp.

GRANDFATHER: Right you are, Eddie.

EDDIE: So we drove to the Saturn Club and went through the receiving line, and at the end… *(As if to a waiter)* My grandfather would like a glass of champagne, please.

GRANDFATHER: Make that a double Old Fashioned.

EDDIE: Wouldn't you like to go into the garden or something, Gramp?

GRANDFATHER: I believe I'd like just to sit here.

EDDIE: *(To audience)* So he sat in the reception room, facing the door watching everyone come in.

GRANDFATHER: You don't need to sit with me, Eddie. Go ask one of those pretty girls to dance.

EDDIE: I'll stay with you, Gramp.

HARVEY: Ah, Eddie. There you are. I need you to show people where to park.

EDDIE: I'm sitting with Gramp.

HARVEY: Eddie: do you remember our little talk about when your father asks you to do something?

EDDIE: Get Tim to help, Dad.

HARVEY: Eddie, I intend to ask you one more time.

GRANDFATHER: Go with your father, Eddie.

EDDIE: I want to stay with you, Gramp.

HARVEY: Eddie. This evening I think you and I can plan on having a major discussion! *(Calling out)* Timmy, I need your help, please.

GRANDFATHER: You're in for it, Eddie.

EDDIE: I know. *(To audience)* And then I made conversation… *(To* GRANDFATHER*)* Gramp, know something? I never understood why salmon swim back to their home pools to die. You've never explained it.

GRANDFATHER: I've read many books about the matter, Eddie. Some people say it's the chemical composition of their home stream. Some say it's the stars. Whatever it is, your salmon knows that the only place he can breed is in his home waters. And I think he knows that by breeding there, he doesn't die at all. But lives on. Through his offspring… And here's your mother.

JANE: Have you had a good time, Father?

GRANDFATHER: I'm still having one.

JANE: Eddie, run tell the parking man to bring around your grandfather's car.

GRANDFATHER: No don't, Eddie.

JANE: Father, you promised.

GRANDFATHER: I've decided to stay at my son's wedding.

JANE: There's been a mix-up, Father. Mother's downstairs.

GRANDFATHER: Can't help that.

JANE: Oh Father, please! I can't do it any more! I can't run between you and Mother any more. I just can't. Please do this for me. Please! I beg you!

GRANDFATHER: All right, Jane. I'll go.

JANE: Eddie, help your grandfather to his car. Use those stairs by the kitchen. I'll hold off Mother.

GRANDFATHER: I don't intend to use the back stairs, Eddie. We'll go the way we came.

EDDIE: *(To audience)* So Gramp and I started across the room. And just then, the band took a break. And guess who walked in? Gram and Uncle Roger. We all met in the middle of the dance floor. Everyone stopped talking. It seemed as if the whole city of Buffalo made this circle around us, and was waiting to see what we'd do. I'll tell you what *I* did. I jumped back, out of the line of fire, like a referee dropping the puck in a hockey face-off. *(Pause)* O.K. Now here's what did *not* happen.

GRANDFATHER: Oh Madeleine, it's great to see you again! You still look gorgeous, even with that gimpy leg. Now leave that grumpy shit, and come with me. I'll give up drinking Old Fashioneds and we'll go trout fishing up at Big Rock, just like the old days. We'll invite our favorite grandson Eddie to come with us.

GRANDMOTHER: That sounds wonderful, Ed. It's over between Roger and me. He's been cranky and disagreeable from the word go. I made a mistake, and I'm sorry. We'll kick Doctor Taubman out of the house on Summer Street, and get your hunting trophies out of the basement of the Science Museum, and things will be just the way they were before I misbehaved.

EDDIE, JANE & HARVEY: Hooray!

(Pause)

EDDIE: Except that didn't happen. And here's something else that didn't happen…

GRANDFATHER: Hey, Roger, you son of a beech-nut-tree! I thought you were my best friend, and then you go and steal my wife right out from under my nose! And now you're living in the house I gave her, and making my grandchildren say uncle, and pretending everything's hunky-dory, when it's not at all, and never will be, because you've ruined my life! So now there's only one thing to do!

GRANDMOTHER: Oh Ed, don't!

GRANDFATHER: Sorry, Madeleine, but I've wanted to do this for a long, long time!

EDDIE: *(To audience)* And then my grandfather hauled off and socked Uncle Roger right in the jaw, and knocked him cold. Then he bowed to my grandmother, and offered her his arm.

GRANDMOTHER: Don't mind if I do, Edward.

EDDIE: Then he led her proudly down the stairs, while everyone cheered and threw rice at them. And when he got to his car, he turned to my grandmother and gave her a big kiss! And I was so excited I even popped my cheek… *(He does.)* Even though it was little juvenile. *(Pause)* Except none of that happened either. *(Pause)* Here's what *did* happen: Gram was humping across the room, concentrating on her bad leg, when she looked up and there was Gramp, right in front of her.

GRANDMOTHER: *(Looking at* GRANDFATHER*)* Oh dear.

EDDIE: That's all she said. Just…

GRANDMOTHER: *(Still looking)* Oh dear.

EDDIE: And Gramp said…

GRANDFATHER: *(Looking at* GRANDMOTHER*)* Hello, Madeleine.

EDDIE: *(To audience)* That's all. And Uncle Roger came up, and gave a slight bow and said, "Hello, Ed." And then, guess what? They all three shook hands! And after that, Gramp went on across the room and down the front stairs, and out the door. I ran after him, just to make sure he was O K. I heard the band start up behind me. I stood in the parking lot and watched my grandfather get into his car, and hunch down behind the wheel, and for the first time he looked like an old man. *(Pause)* So I went back and danced with Margie Woodrich.

***

JANE: *(On telephone)* Eddie? Is this a terrible time to telephone?

EDDIE: *(On telephone)* No, no. I just put the kids to bed, and Margie's out at a P T A meeting.

JANE: I've got sad news. Your grandmother died last night.

EDDIE: Oh gosh…I'm so sorry… What of?

JANE: Everything, apparently. I think she just ran out of steam. Sitting out there, year after year, at Roger's beck and call…

EDDIE: How's he doing?

JANE: Roger? Going strong. I hear he's now involved with Mother's trained nurse.

EDDIE: We'll drive up for the funeral.

JANE: Would you? We need a few warm bodies. Your sister can't leave Los Angeles. She promised to go to some Jewish thing with her in-laws.

EDDIE: A bar mitzvah?

JANE: That sounds right. Anyway, Timmy can't come all the way from Korea. And of course poor Freddy won't be here.

EDDIE: *(To audience)* Uncle Freddy was shot down over Germany in 1943. Teresa married some guy from New Orleans and lives in Seattle.

(The actors may look at each other more during this final section.)

EDDIE: *(To* JANE*)* It was a nice funeral, Mom.

HARVEY: Small, I'll say that.

JANE: Mother left this for you, Eddie.

GRANDMOTHER: …to my dear grandson Eddie I leave my own personal copy of *Wuthering Heights*, by Emily Bronte…

HARVEY: The leather's cracking. It should be rubbed every year with neat's foot oil.

JANE: Where do you buy neat's foot oil?

HARVEY: You can't, any more.

EDDIE: Look. Gram wrote stuff in the margins.

GRANDMOTHER: Oh my! …How true! …How beautiful! …This is heart-breaking!

HARVEY: *Wuthering Heights*. What a sad book to leave someone.

EDDIE: You're thinking of the movie, Pop. The book ends happily. The younger generation gets married and picks up the pieces.

JANE: Keeping the wagons in a circle. Sounds very Buffalo.

EDDIE: *(To audience)* My grandfather died a few months after Gram. It's as if he didn't want to live in the world without her.

JANE: He just stopped eating.

HARVEY: Though he didn't stop drinking Old Fashioneds.

GRANDFATHER: …To Eddie, my grandson and namesake, I leave my three-piece, eight-and-one-half foot, six-ounce Leonard bamboo fly-rod, along with my dry flies and my jacking paddle from Big Rock…

HARVEY: The bamboo's cracked, I'm afraid.

EDDIE: I'll hang it on the wall. Next to the paddle.

JANE: I'm sorry Margie and the children couldn't come up this time.

EDDIE: They didn't know him.

JANE: They missed something.

EDDIE: I agree.

GRANDFATHER: Three logs, Eddie. Properly placed. And your fire will last indefinitely….

JANE: It'll be just us at the graveside, then. The new man from Trinity Church will say a few words.

EDDIE: *(To audience)* Gramp and Gram are both buried in Forest Lawn. Gram is buried with the Woodriches. Gramp is quite close by, below Old E G and Old S S.

HARVEY: *(To audience)* It's a magnificent cemetery, beautifully designed by Frederick Law Olmstead, just as the city was hitting its stride.

JANE: *(To audience)* There they all are, shaded by one of the last stands of American elms.

HARVEY: *(To audience)* A spectacular tree, which once vaulted the principal avenues of Buffalo—or Beau Fleuve, as we were originally called.

JANE: After the beautiful Niagara River.

HARVEY: Which I can see from my office, now they've torn down the old grain elevators. *(To* EDDIE*)* I read in *Time* we're now the fifty-second largest city in the United States.

JANE: Poor old Buffalo.

EDDIE: *(To* JANE*)* We should have buried Gramp next to Buck and Earl, near Big Rock. He was at his best up there.

JANE: He should be with his family. Family comes first. You might remind your children of that.

EDDIE: I hear you, Mother. *(To audience)* And I did.

(Slow fade)

END OF PLAY

CHRONOLOGY

SEASON & YEAR	EVENT	EDDIE'S AGE
Spring, 1938	ROGER *moves in*	8
Fall, 1938	ROGER & GRAM *marry*	8
Summer, 1939	*Trip to Big Rock*	9
	Pool and court built	
Spring, 1940	*Running the gauntlet*	10
Summer, 1940	*Moving* GRAMP	10
Fall, 1940	GRAM *falls off horse*	10
Winter, 1941	*Valentine's Day*	11
Spring, 1941	Wuthering Heights	11
December 7, 1941	*Pearl Harbor*	11
December 25, 1941	*Mrs Mitchell*	11
Spring 1942	*Farewell Lunch*	12
	Spring Dance	
	Freddy's wedding	
Coda, 1960's		30s